ENERGY
Makes Things Happen

by Kimberly Brubaker Bradley • illustrated by Paul Meisel

HarperCollins Publishers

To the Smith College Department of Chemistry (1985–1989),
who taught me that science was wonder and delight: Lâle Aka Burk,
David Bickar, Maria Bickar, George Fleck, Dorothy Hamilton, Kenneth Hellman,
Robert Linck, Thomas Lowry, Sharon Palmer,
Stuart Rosenfeld, and Virginia White
—K.B.B.

Special thanks to Louis A. Bloomfield, professor of physics,
the University of Virginia, for his time and expert review

The *Let's-Read-and-Find-Out Science* book series was originated by Dr. Franklyn M. Branley, Astronomer Emeritus and former Chairman of the American Museum–Hayden Planetarium, and was formerly co-edited by him and Dr. Roma Gans, Professor Emeritus of Childhood Education, Teachers College, Columbia University. Text and illustrations for each of the books in the series are checked for accuracy by an expert in the relevant field. For more information about Let's-Read-and-Find-Out Science books, write to HarperCollins Children's Books, 1350 Avenue of the Americas, New York, NY 10019, or visit our website at www.letsreadandfindout.com.

Library of Congress Cataloging-in-Publication Data
Bradley, Kimberly Brubaker.
Energy makes things happen / by Kimberly Brubaker Bradley ; illustrated by Paul Meisel.
p.   cm.—(Let's-read-and-find-out science. Stage 2)
Summary: Simple language and humorous illustrations show how energy comes originally from the sun and can be transferred from one thing to another.
ISBN 0-06-028908-2 — ISBN 0-06-445213-1 (pbk.) — ISBN 0-06-028909-0 (lib. bdg.)
1. Force and energy—Juvenile literature.   2. Energy transfer—Juvenile literature. [1. Force and energy.   2. Power resources.   3. Energy transfer.]
I. Meisel, Paul, ill.   II. Title.   III. Series.   QC73.4 .B73   2003   531'.6—dc21   2001039520   CIP   AC

Typography by Elynn Cohen   1 2 3 4 5 6 7 8 9 10   ❖   First Edition

ENERGY
Makes Things Happen

The sun shines in the sky. Two children run with a kite. A boy sails a boat across a pond. A girl hits a baseball. A family cooks hot dogs on a campfire. A big rock sits high on a hill.

All these things have different kinds of energy.

Energy makes things happen. It can make things hot or bright or loud. It can make things move. Energy can be used to do work. There are many different kinds of energy. When the sun shines, it gives us light. The sun also gives us heat. Both heat and light are kinds of energy.

When you run or jump or hop or skip, that's energy too. Everything that moves uses energy.

Energy is transferred from one thing to another. When a boy throws a baseball, he transfers energy from his arm to the ball. Then the ball can move through the air. (The more energy he gives the ball, the faster it goes!)

When a girl swings a bat, she transfers energy from her arms to the bat. When the bat hits the ball, the energy in the bat goes into the ball and sends it flying.

Wind is air that moves—it's air with
energy. The energy from wind lifts kites
into the sky. It makes windmills go around
and hot-air balloons soar. Wind energy
sails sailboats across a pond.

11

Things that release energy as they are burned are called fuels.
Gasoline, oil, and wood are all fuels. When we put gasoline into
a car, we are putting fuel into it. As the car runs, its engine burns
the gasoline. The gasoline gets used up. The energy from the
gasoline makes the car go forward.

When we build a campfire to cook hot dogs, we are burning wood fuel to turn its stored energy into heat energy for the hot dogs.

But the hot dogs are also a kind of fuel! Our bodies need energy, and they get it from the food we eat. Strawberries, rutabagas, potato salad, milk, popcorn, tuna fish, and hot dogs—everything we eat gets used up by our bodies.

SPECIAL

Our food is the fuel that gives us the energy to run and play.

Food gives us energy to do our work.

You may not think a glass of milk contains energy. Milk is not moving or doing work. It's not hot. It doesn't give off light. But milk has energy stored inside it. All fuels do.

Remember the rock on the hill? It has energy inside it too. It's not hot or moving, and it isn't a fuel—you can't eat it or drink it or burn it. BUT—if you gave the rock a tiny push, it would roll all the way down the hill. It would turn its stored energy into moving energy.

A rock at the bottom of a hill does not have stored energy to turn into moving energy. If you push it, it doesn't fall anywhere. But if you roll the rock all the way to the top of the hill, you give it the energy to fall back down the hill. The energy you use to push it up the hill stays with the rock, waiting, so that eventually the rock can fall back down the hill.

The rock might sit on the hill for a long time. It can't fall back down until someone or something gives it a little push. Then it can fall a long way. Many things need a little bit of energy to help them give off a lot of energy. A candle stores energy, but it doesn't burn until it's lit. A carrot stores energy, but it can't give it out until you eat it.

We can see how energy got into the rock—someone pushed it up the hill. But how did energy get into the carrot? Or into gasoline, or into any of our fuels?

Most of our energy comes from the sun. The sun gives off so much energy that even though it is very far away, a lot of its heat and light reach the earth.

The energy from the sun makes plants grow. So the carrot contains energy from the sun. The sun's energy makes grass grow. Cows eat the grass and get energy to make milk.

So the milk and the cows contain energy from the sun. We drink milk and get the energy to take care of the cows! And to push rocks up hills. The energy we get from our food first came from the sun.

The energy in gasoline first came from the sun too. Gasoline is made from a fossil fuel. Fossil fuels are made from the remains of plants and animals that lived long ago. The sun gave these plants and animals energy to grow.

Coal, natural gas, and oil are fossil fuels.

The sun warms us and gives us light. It warms the air and creates the wind. The sun gives off a lot of energy.

Energy never disappears. It can move from one object—such as a baseball bat—to another—such as a ball. Energy can move from the sun to a carrot to a child to a rock. It can flow from light into a plant, from a plant into a fuel, from a fuel into the movement of a car going down the street—but energy never goes away.

That's good, because we need lots of energy. Without it, we couldn't move! We wouldn't have light or heat—we wouldn't grow. Nothing could. Without energy, we wouldn't have anything. We need energy to make things happen!

Moving Cars

Energy can be transferred from one object to another. Here's how you can see it happen.

First, get two small toy cars (blocks or marbles would work fine, too, but cars are easier to use). Set one toy car by itself in the middle of a hard surface, like a smooth floor or a table. Now take the second car and give it a push so that it rolls into the back of the first car. (Don't hold on to the second car.) *Bam!*

What happens to the first car? Does it move? Did the motion require energy? Where did the energy come from? What happens to the second car? Where did ITS energy come from?

Now get a third car. Line the first two up so they are touching, back to front. Take the third car and roll it into the back of the second car just like you did before.

What happens? Which cars move? Which moves the farthest?

The energy from the moving car gets transferred to the nonmoving car. When there are three cars, the energy is transferred from the first car to the second, and then from the second to the third—all faster than you can blink!

Back to the Sun

Think of something—anything—that uses energy. Can you trace this energy back to the sun? Pretend you are playing baseball. Your body would have to move, and that would require energy. Where does your body get the energy?

From the food you eat. Let's say you ate a toasted cheese sandwich for lunch right before you played baseball. Where did the energy in the sandwich come from?

The cheese was made from milk, the bread from wheat. Wheat is a plant—it gets its energy to grow from the sun. Cows make milk, but of course it takes energy for them to do so. Where do they get the energy? From the food they eat. What do they eat? Grass. Where does the grass get the energy to grow? From the sun. So the energy it takes for you to play baseball originally came from the sun.

This is a fun game to play. If you think hard enough, you'll find out that almost all the energy we use on earth first came from the sun.